GA
CENGAGE Learning

Drama for Students, Volume 3

Staff

Editorial: David M. Galens, *Editor*. Terry Browne, Christopher Busiel, Clare Cross, Tom Faulkner, John Fiero, David M. Galens, Carole Hamilton, Sheri Metzger, Daniel Moran, Terry Nienhuis, William P. Wiles, Joanne Woolway, Etta Worthington, *Entry Writers*. Elizabeth Cranston, Kathleen J. Edgar, Jennifer Gariepy, Dwayne D. Hayes, Kurt Kuban, Joshua Kondek, Tom Ligotti, Scot Peacock, Patti Tippett, Pam Zuber, *Contributing Editors*. James Draper, *Managing Editor*. Diane Telgen, *"For Students" Line Coordinator*. Jeffery Chapman, *Programmer/Analyst*.

Research: Victoria B. Cariappa, *Research Team Manager*. Andy Malonis, Barb McNeil, *Research Specialists*. Julia C. Daniel, Tamara C. Nott, Tracie A. Richardson, Cheryl L. Warnock, *Research Associates*. Phyllis P. Blackman, Jeffrey D. Daniels,

Corrine A. Stocker, *Research Assistants*.

Permissions: Susan M. Trosky, *Permissions Manager*. Kimberly F. Smilay, *Permissions Specialist*. Steve Cusack and Kelly A. Quin, *Permissions Associates*.

Production: Mary Beth Trimper, *Production Director*. Evi Seoud, *Assistant Production Manager*. Shanna Heilveil, *Production Assistant*.

Graphic Services: Randy Bassett, *Image Database Supervisor*. Robert Duncan and Michael Logusz, *Imaging Specialists*. Pamela A. Reed, *Photography Coordinator*. Gary Leach, *Macintosh Artist*.

Product Design: Cynthia Baldwin, *Product Design Manager*. Cover Design: Michelle DiMercurio, *Art Director*. Page Design: Pamela A. E. Galbreath, *Senior Art Director*.

editors or publisher. Errors brought to the attention of the publisher and verified to the satisfaction of the publisher will be corrected in future editions.

Copyright © 1998
Gale Research
835 Penobscot Building
645 Griswold
Detroit, MI 48226-4094

ISBN 0-7876-2752-6
ISSN 1094-9232

Printed in the United States of America
10 9 8 7 6 5 4 3 2

Fences

August Wilson

1983

Introduction

The first staged reading of August Wilson's play *Fences* occurred in 1983 at the Eugene O'Neill Theatre Center's National Playwright's Conference. Wilson's drama opened at the Yale Repertory Theatre in 1985 and on Broadway at the 46th Street Theatre in 1987. *Fences* was well-received, winning four Antionette ("Tony") Perry Awards, including best play. The work also won the New York Drama Critics' Circle Award, the Pulitzer Prize, and the

John Gassner Outer Critics' Circle Award. Wilson was also selected as Artist of the Year by the *Chicago Tribune*.

Fences was a huge success with both critics and viewers, and it drew black audiences to the theatre in much larger numbers than usual. Because the play had four years of pre-production development before it opened on Broadway, Wilson had a chance to tighten and revise the action, watching his characters mature into lifelike creations. James Earl Jones played the role of Troy in the first staging of *Fences* on Broadway. Jones—and many black audience members—recognized and identified with Wilson's use of language to define his black characters. In an interview with Heather Henderson in *Theater*, Jones stated that "Few writers can capture dialect as dialogue in a manner as interesting and accurate as August's."

Reviewers also noted Wilson's ability to create believable characters. In his review for *Newsweek*, Allan Wallach noted that it is the men who dominate the script and bring it to life—singling out Jones, whom Wallach noted, is at his best "in the bouts of drinking and bantering." It is Jones's performance that creates "a rich portrait of a man who scaled down his dreams to fit inside his run-down yard." Clive Barnes, writing for the *New York Post*, said that Wilson provides "the strongest, most passionate American dramatic writing since Tennessee Williams" (*Cat on a Hot Tin Roof*). *Fences*, said Barnes, "gave me one of the richest experiences I have ever had in the theater."

Author Biography

August Wilson was born Frederick August Kittel, on April 27, 1945, in a ghetto area of Pittsburgh, Pennsylvania, known as "The Hill." Wilson's white father, a German baker named August Kittel, abandoned the family when Wilson was a child. Wilson's mother, Daisy Wilson Kittel, worked as a cleaning woman to raise her six children. Later, after Wilson's mother had remarried, his stepfather moved the family to a white neighborhood where Wilson was subjected to unbridled racism. At age 15, Wilson dropped out of school after being falsely accused of plagiarism; after that episode, he continued his education on his own, with periods of extensive reading at the public library.

Wilson began his career writing poetry and short stories but switched to drama in 1978 when he was invited to write plays for a black theatre in Minneapolis-St. Paul. Several fellowships enabled Wilson to concentrate on writing plays as a fulltime venture. Although his early efforts, *Fullerton Street* (1980), *Black Bart and the Sacred Hills* (1981), and *Jitney* (1982) received little attention, he gained recognition with his 1984 play, *Ma Rainey's Black Bottom*, which was accepted for a staged reading at the Eugene O'Neill Theatre Center's National Playwright's Conference in 1982. The following year, *Fences* was also presented at the O'Neill conference and in 1986 *Joe Turner's Come and Gone* became Wilson's third play to be produced at the conference.

Each of these plays followed their initial readings at the O'Neill with productions at the Yale Repertory Theatre and later stagings on Broadway. In 1987, *The Piano Lesson* opened at the Yale Repertory Theatre; *Two Trains Running* followed three years later. Wilson's *Seven Guitars* opened at the Goodman Theatre in Chicago in 1995. Wilson has stated that he envisions his plays as representative of the black experience in America, since each play is set in a different decade.

Wilson married for the first time in 1969, but the marriage ended after three years and the birth of a daughter, Sakina Ansari. He married for a second time in 1981; this marriage ended in 1990. Wilson has won several honors for his writing, including the New York Drama Critics' Circle Award, an Antionette ("Tony") Perry Award, and a Pulitzer Prize for *Fences; The Piano Lesson* was also awarded a Pulitzer Prize in 1990. Several of his other works have been nominated for Tony Awards.

Plot Summary

Act I, scene i

The play opens with Troy and Bono engaged in their usual Friday night ritual of drinking and talking. Troy has made a formal complaint to his bosses that only white men are permitted to drive the garbage trucks for the waste disposal company at which both men work. The two men finish their discussion of work, and Bono asks Troy about a woman, Alberta, he suspects Troy of seeing. Troy denies that he would risk losing his wife, Rose, but Bono does not give up so easily and reminds Troy that he has been seen at Alberta's house when he said he was elsewhere.

Their conversation is interrupted by Troy's wife, Rose, who enters the yard. Their conversation about where to shop is interrupted by Lyons's entrance. Lyons is Troy's son by a previous marriage. He has come by because he knows that his father gets paid on Fridays; he is in need of a loan and asks his father for ten dollars. Troy pointedly notes that Lyons needs to get a job. Lyons's reply is that his father had no hand in raising him, and thus, he has no right to chastise or complain about how Lyons is living his life. Rose intervenes and gives Lyons the money.

Act I, scene ii

Rose is hanging clothes on the line. Troy enters and they begin to banter about Rose's habit of playing numbers (a form of betting, like a lottery). Troy thinks it foolish and a waste of money, but Rose finds this little bit of gambling to be a harmless diversion that occasionally offers a small reward. Their conversation moves to Troy's inquiry about the presence of their son, Cory. At that moment, Troy's brother, Gabriel, enters the yard. He is singing and carrying a bowl of discarded fruit and vegetables that he has picked up and is now attempting to sell. Gabriel was injured in the war and is now mentally disabled. Gabriel is worried that his older brother is angry that he has moved out and into his own place. As Gabriel exits, still singing, Rose reassures Troy that he has done all he can to care for his brother.

Act I, scene iii

Four hours later, Rose is taking the dried clothes down from the line. Cory enters and is directed by his mother to get into the house and start the chores that he ignored when he went to football practice.

Troy enters the yard and after hearing that Cory is home, yells for his son to come out of the house. An argument ensues between father and son about Cory's concentration on football at the expense of his other obligations: school, chores, and a parttime job he has just quit. Troy demands complete control over Cory and insists that he quit football. Cory responds by asking his father why he doesn't like his son. Troy evades a direct answer, and, instead, he replies that his son is provided with a home and food because he, Troy, fulfills his responsibility to his family. The confrontation ends with Troy telling Cory to get back down to the supermarket and get his job back.

When Rose returns, Troy explains that he wants his son to do better than his father and to have a better job than that of a garbage man. Rose tries to soften Troy by reminding him that he missed his chance to be a professional athlete because he was too old, but Troy is unwilling to admit that she is right. The scene ends with Troy's declaration that he simply moves through life, existing from one Friday night to the next.

Act I, scene iv

It is another Friday night, two weeks later, and Cory is on his way to play football. He ignores Rose when she confronts him about the chores he has left undone and states that he'll do them later. Troy and Bono enter the yard after Cory leaves, and Troy announces that he has been made a driver. At that moment Lyons comes to repay the money he borrowed two weeks ago. Most of this scene is devoted to the issue of Cory's future.

Troy launches into an autobiographical story that explains much of his behavior. The audience learns about Troy's brutal father and that he has been on his own since he was fourteen. The audience also learns that Troy spent fifteen years in jail and that is where he met Bono. The scene ends with a confrontation between Troy and Cory, who has just entered the yard. Troy accuses Cory of lying and orders him to get his old job back and quit the football team.

Act II, scene i

Troy has just returned from bailing Gabriel out of jail. Bono is with him, and, in response to his friend's concern about Rose, Troy admits that he has been seeing another woman and that she is going to have his baby. Rose enters the yard as Bono is leaving. Troy realizes that with a child coming, he must accept responsibility for what he has done. He tells Rose that he is to be the father to another woman's child. His response to her anger and pain is an admission that the other woman offers an escape from his responsibilities. She makes him forget the endless repetition of his life for a few moments. The scene ends in a confrontation between Rose, Troy, and Cory that stops just short of physical violence.

Act II, scene ii

It is six months later, and it is clear that the relationship between Rose and Troy has been severed. Although Troy gives his wife his paycheck, he is spending almost all his time with Alberta. Troy and Rose argue, but their fight is interrupted by a phone call telling them that the baby has been born but that the mother has died. The scene ends with Troy yelling at death, vowing to build a fence around his house and those he loves to keep death away.

Act II, scene iii

Troy returns with the infant, who he has named Raynell, and he and Rose agree that she will raise the child, who should not be punished for her parents' sins.

Act II, scene iv

It is two months later and much has changed. Cory has graduated and is looking for a job, but Lyons tells him that jobs are scarce. Rose is busy with her church activities; she has found something to fill the space within that Troy had occupied before his deception. A brief conversation between Troy and Bono reveals that the two friends have drifted apart. Troy is a driver and Bono is still picking up the trash on a different route. After Bono leaves, Cory returns and there is a final argument between father and son. Clearly Cory blames Troy for his mother's pain and for his own disappointment. The argument turns violent when Cory attempts to strike at Troy with a baseball bat; he misses and Troy seizes the bat but stops just short of striking his son. In the end, Cory leaves the house for good, and Troy ends the scene with a taunt for death to come.

Act II, scene v

It is seven years later and the family has gathered for Troy's funeral. Cory arrives in his marine uniform. When he states that he will not go to Troy's funeral, his mother convinces him that he has an obligation to go. But it is the singing of Troy's favorite song with the child, Raynell, that really convinces Cory to put the past behind him. The scene ends with all the principal characters in the yard. Gabriel announces he has come to blow the trumpet for Troy's admittance to Heaven through St. Peter's gate. The horn's mouthpiece is broken, however, and instead Gabriel begins to dance and howl as the stage darkens.

Characters

Jim Bono

Bono is Troy Maxson's closest friend. They met while in prison and spent fifteen years together locked inside. Troy has been the leader whom Bono has willingly followed. They work together hauling garbage until Troy is promoted to driver. That event, combined with Troy's preoccupation with his pregnant mistress, serves to create the first serious discord between the two men in nearly thirty-four years of friendship. Bono is very concerned with Troy's dalliance with another woman and the risk it poses to his friend's marriage. Jim's wife, Lucille, is never seen on stage, but he speaks of her with obvious affection and admiration; she has tamed his wanderlust. Bono's positive relationship with Lucille demonstrates that a man has the ability to change the direction of his life.

Cory Maxson

Cory is the Maxsons' teenage son. When the play opens he is being actively recruited for a college football scholarship. His father feels that he is spending too much time at practice and ignoring his other responsibilities. Cory represents all the possibilities his father never had, but he also represents Troy's unmet dreams. Troy wants his son to achieve a future that does not include hauling garbage. Yet the father is unwilling to let the son attempt something that may bring him success; Troy is afraid that the world of white-dominated sports will only break Cory's heart.

When Cory quits his job to concentrate on football, his father retaliates by going to the coach and forbidding Cory to play. After a particularly heated confrontation, Cory leaves home. At the play's end, he returns after an absence of seven years for his father's funeral. Cory has spent the last six years as a Marine, but he is now considering a new direction that includes marriage and a new job. Initially he does not want to attend his father's funeral, the chasm is too wide, and he believes his controlling father never loved him. He eventually realizes that he must put the past behind him, forgive his father, and attend the funeral.

Gabriel Maxson

Gabriel is Troy's brother. Troy has helped care for Gabriel since World War II during which his brother received a debilitating head injury. Gabriel's mental capacity has been diminished by the injury and left him believing that he is the archangel Gabriel. Troy used Gabriel's disability settlement to buy the house in which the family lives, and he continues to receive a part of Gabriel's monthly benefit checks as rent. When the play opens, Gabriel has just moved into his own lodgings. His life is filled with his singing and his expressed wait for St. Peter to call upon Gabriel to open the gates of heaven.

After bailing Gabriel out of jail several times, Troy finally has him committed to a mental hospital. At the play's end, it is Gabriel who brings some resolution as he calls for the gate of heaven to open and admit Troy. Gabriel attempts to blow a trumpet to herald Troy into heaven, finds that the mouthpiece is broken, and begins a jumping about and howling as the stage darkens.

Lyons Maxson

Lyons is Troy's thirty-four-year-old son from a previous marriage; he was raised by his mother after Troy was sent to jail, and he has little respect for his father's advice. He does, however, have need of his father's money, frequently arriving at the house on Troy's paydays. Lyons hopes for a career as a musician and is disinterested in any work that would interfere with his goal. Consequently, he is unemployed and is supported by his wife, Bonnie. Lyons knows little about his father, but when he hears that his father has been on his own since he was fourteen, Lyons is finally impressed enough to pay attention as his father speaks.

Raynell Maxson

Raynell is the child Troy fathered with his mistress, Alberta. When Alberta dies giving birth, he brings the three-day old infant home for Rose to raise. She is seven years old when her father dies, but she has come to represent all the family's hopes for a better future. In the final scene, it is Raynell and Cory's singing of their father's favorite song that helps heal the pain of Cory's angry memories of his father.

Rose Maxson

Rose is Troy's wife of eighteen years. She is ten years younger than him and a strong woman who is devoted to her husband. Her devotion ends, however, when Troy tells her of his affair with Alberta and his impending fatherhood. Rose wants the fence built around their house so that she can keep her family safe within its confines. She tries to mediate the conflicts that arise between Troy and his sons. It is Rose who loans money to Lyons, and it is Rose who tries to soften Troy's unconditional control over Cory's life. She is deeply wounded by Troy's affair and although they continue living in the same house, their loving relationship as husband and wife is over. Rose agrees to raise the child, Raynell, because she does not believe that the child should suffer for the sin of her parents. She substitutes religion for the companionship of marriage, and by the time Raynell is born, Rose has become an active member of her church. It is Rose who calls for family unity and healing at the play's end; she urges all the family members and friends to forgive and remember the good things about Troy.

Troy Maxson

Troy is the principal character. He is fifty-three when the play begins. He has led a hard life, raised by an abusive father and later jailed for robbery and murder. During the fifteen years he spent in jail, Troy became an accomplished baseball player. But after his release from jail Troy was too old to play in the newly-integrated major leagues. He is bitter and resentful at the opportunities lost because of the color of his skin and is desperate to protect Cory from the same sort of disappointment. Troy lives in the past and fails to recognize that the world has changed. His father was brutal and controlling, and although Troy loves Cory, he knows of no other way to bring up a son. Thus he repeats the mistakes of the previous generation.

Troy feels a need to control every element of his life and even declares that he will fight death if necessary. His affair with Alberta represents his attempt to escape the responsibility he feels for wife, son, and home. Unable to open up to those that he loves, Troy keeps much of his emotion inside, building imaginary fences between himself and his family and friends. While he realizes the financial responsibility of being the head of a family, he fails to grasp the emotional part of the job. Troy finally succeeds in isolating himself from his wife, his brother, his sons, and his friend.

Themes

Death

In *Fences*, death is a character. Rather than the elusive unknown, death becomes an object that Troy attempts to battle. The unfinished fence that Troy is building around his home is completed only when Troy feels threatened by death. In one of the stories he tells, Troy relates how he once wrestled with death and won. When the simmering conflict between Troy and Cory finally erupts and the boy leaves his father's house for good, it is death that Troy calls upon to do battle. And in the last scene, it is death that unites the family and helps bring resolution to their lives. When the family meets again at Troy's funeral, they are finally given a chance to bury the pain and disappointments of their lives.

Duty and Responsibility

Troy Maxson is a man who assumes the responsibilities of father, husband, and provider. In addition, he looks after his disabled brother, Gabriel. Though he faces these responsibilities, he is also overwhelmed by them, seeking escape when it is offered to him. When it is revealed that Alberta, the other woman that Troy has been seeing, is pregnant, Troy responds that he is not ducking the responsibility of what he has done. He accepts the obligation he owes to both his wife and his mistress.

When Rose asks why Troy needed another woman, his reply is that Alberta was an escape from his responsibilities. She did not have a roof that needed fixing; her house was a place where he could forget that he was someone's husband, someone's father, someone's employee. Troy feels the weight of responsibility so heavily that he can see only endless weeks of labor, endless paychecks to be cashed, endless Fridays blending into one another. When Alberta dies giving birth, Troy assumes responsibility for the infant and brings her to his home. In turn, Rose agrees to raise and care for the child. In the end it is the responsibility each member of the family feels toward the others that brings resolution to the story.

Fences

Fences represent many different things in Wilson's drama. Rose thinks the partially built fence around the house will keep her loved ones safe inside. But for Troy, the fence is a way to keep unwanted intruders out. After Alberta's death, he completes the fence as a means to keep death from entering and hurting his loved ones. When Troy played baseball, he was never content to hit the ball into the stands. His hits always had to go over the fence. And yet, Troy builds a fence around Cory to keep him from his goals and desires. Troy's efforts at controlling his son create an imaginary fence that keeps the boy separate from his family for seven years. There are similar fences between Troy and his loved ones; in one way or another he has kept them separated from a part of himself.

When Troy tells his life story, it is a tale of penitentiary walls behind which he was a prisoner for fifteen years. Bono was also confined within these walls. By Act II, the walls of a mental hospital will separate Gabriel from his family. Troy also sees white America having a fence that keeps blacks contained, apart from the good life that whites enjoy. It is the fence that kept him from realizing his dreams and the fence that makes blacks garbage collectors while whites advance to better positions such as driver.

In the sense of physical setting, the fence around Troy's house also contains the action of the play. Everything takes place in the yard; all of the scenes and the dialogue occur within the boundaries of the fence.

Friendship

The friendship between Troy and Bono is the first relationship shown in the play. Their conversations provide a glimpse into Troy's thoughts. Bono has been following Troy's lead since they met in prison more than thirty years earlier. Troy has been a role model for Bono, but Bono serves as a conscience for Troy. It is Bono who first alerts the audience to Troy's extramarital affair, and it is Bono who questions the wisdom of Troy's actions. The friendship is tested when Troy is promoted to driver and put on another route. When questioned about his absence from Troy's house, Bono replies that it is the new job that keeps them apart. But there is also a hint that Troy's betrayal of Rose has changed the dynamics of their friendship.

Limitations and Opportunities

At the heart of Troy's unhappiness is his disappointment at not being able to play professional baseball. Troy became an accomplished ball player while in prison. He was good enough to play in the Negro leagues, but his true desire was to play major league ball. Troy felt he was excluded because, at the time, black players were still not accepted, but the story is more complex than Troy wants to believe. The fifteen years that Troy spent in prison made him too old for the major leagues. Troy ignores this argument, since to acknowledge that he was too old is to accept partial responsibility for not being able to play; it was his own actions that led to a fifteen year prison term, a period during which his youth slipped away. It is easier for Troy to blame a system that discriminates against black players than to admit that he lacked either the talent or the youth to play major league baseball.

Topics for Further Study

- What is the nature of the conflict between Cory and Troy? Research the options for black athletes who were recruited by colleges in the 1950s. Do you find that Troy's reservations about Cory's future as a ballplayer have merit?

- Troy cannot read and so the oral tradition is an important means of communication for him. He tells his life story in Act I, scene iv. But he also tells part of his story through song. Research the role of storytelling as a part of the black experience. Consider also how the oral tradition has been replaced in many cultures by the printed page. Do you think that the oral tradition is a disappearing part of the American cultural experience?

- In *Fences*, Troy's description of the devil eventually evolves into a description of a white salesman who cheats his black customers because they are too afraid to question his pronouncements, and thus, they allow themselves to be cheated. Examine the commercial relationship between whites and blacks in the 1950s. Is Troy's cynicism justified by the facts?

- Early in Wilson's play, music and athletics are singled out the best opportunities for young black men to escape the ghetto existence of black urban life. Later, Cory joins the Marines, but is this an escape? In 1964, the United States is beginning a build-up of military strength in Vietnam, it will evolve into a war that will eventually be lost. What exactly did the military offer young black men? Research the role of the black soldier in Vietnam and consider if the percentage of blacks who died in that war represented an unequal sacrifice of life.

Troy's son, Cory, also has the opportunity for a

better life through athletics. But Troy is so bitter over his own lack of opportunity that he holds his son back from any success he might achieve. When Cory is recruited for a college football scholarship, it is his father who forbids Cory to play. Troy is unable to accept that his son might succeed where he had failed—and Cory accuses his father of just such a motivation. But it is more than a desire to control Cory's success that is at the heart of Troy's actions. He truly fails to see that the world has changed in the past twenty years. Black men are now playing professional sports with white men. The restrictions that kept the two races apart athletically have eased. A football scholarship would mean more than playing a sport; it would be an opportunity for education and a chance to advance to a better world.

Race and Racism

In a story that Troy tells in the play, the devil is represented as a white business owner who takes advantage of his black customers. The setting for *Fences* is just before the racial tensions of the 1960s erupt. Troy is a garbage man. He has noticed that only white men are promoted to driver, and, although he possesses no driver's license, Troy complains about the injustice of a system that favors one race while excluding another. Because he has complained, Troy is promoted, but the result is that he no longer works with his friends and the camaraderie of the workplace is lost. Troy also feels that his dream to play professional baseball was destroyed because he was a black player in a white world. Because he has spent a lifetime being excluded, Troy cannot see any advantage for his son when college recruiters come to watch Cory play football. Troy cannot trust the white man, the devil, and so, he forbids his son to play football.

Act

A major division in a drama. In Greek plays the sections of the drama signified by the appearance of the chorus and were usually divided into five acts. This is the formula for most serious drama from the Greeks to the Romans to Elizabethan playwrights like William Shakespeare. The five acts denote the structure of dramatic action. They are exposition, complication, climax, falling action, and catastrophe. The five act structure was followed until the nineteenth century when Henrik Ibsen *(A Doll's House)* combined some of the acts. *Fences* is a two act play. The exposition and complication are combined in the first act when the audience learns of Troy's affair with another woman and of the conflict between father and son, the role sports plays in each man's life. The climax occurs in the second act when Troy must admit to having fathered a child with his mistress. The climax to the father-son friction also occurs in the second act when the conflict between Troy and Cory escalates, and Cory leaves his father's home for good. The catastrophe also occurs in this act when the players assemble for Troy's funeral and Cory is finally able to deal with his resentment and accept his father's failings.

Setting

The time, place, and culture in which the action of the play takes place is called the setting. The elements of setting may include geographic location, physical or mental environments, prevailing cultural attitudes, or the historical time in which the action takes place. The location for *Fences* is an urban city in 1957 America. The action occurs over a period of several months and then jumps ahead seven years for the last scene. The action is further reduced to one set, the yard of the Maxson home.

Character

A person in a dramatic work. The actions of each character are what constitute the story. Character can also include the idea of a particular individual's morality. Characters can range from simple stereotypical figures to more complex multi-faceted ones. Characters may also be defined by personality traits, such as the rogue or the damsel in distress. "Characterization" is the process of creating a lifelike person from an author's imagination. To accomplish this, the author provides the character with personality traits that help define who he will be and how he will behave in a given situation. For instance, in the beginning of *Fences* Troy seems to accept the responsibilities he has acquired. He appears content with his marriage and comfortable in providing for his family and caring for Gabriel. As the action progresses, however, it becomes clear that Troy yearns for escape from these responsibilities. He finds this escape with Alberta but at the cost of his marriage.

Conflict

The conflict is the issue(s) to be resolved in the play. It usually occurs between two characters, but it can also occur between a character and society (as it does in Arthur Miller's *The Crucible*). Conflict serves to create tension in a plot—it is often the motivating force that drive a plot. For instance, in *Fences* there is a clear conflict between Cory's desire to play footfall and the disappointments that his father felt when his dreams of success in professional sports were never realized. There is also conflict between Troy and his wife when she discovers that he has fathered a child with another woman. And finally, Troy's disappointment in sports represents the conflict between a largely whitedominated organization, professional sports, and a talented black man who feels he has been cheated and deprived of success. This conflict provides one of the fences that isolates black athletes from opportunities available to white Americans.

Metaphor

Metaphor is an analogy that identifies one object with another and ascribes to the first object the qualities of the second. For example, the fence is a metaphor for the walls that confine Troy and Bono to prison. There are fences (though unseen) between Troy and his family. It is also a metaphor for the white society that confines blacks and restricts their opportunities. In this drama, baseball is also a metaphor for Troy's life. His successes are hits over the fence, but his failures are strike-outs.

Plot

This term refers to the pattern of events. Generally plots should have a beginning, a middle, and a conclusion, but they may also be a series of episodes connected together. Basically, the plot provides the author with the means to explore primary themes. Students are often confused between the two terms; but themes explore ideas, and plots simply relate what happens in a very obvious manner. Thus the plot of *Fences* is the story of a black family divided by the loss and anger of past and present disappointments. But the themes are those of family unity and love and racial intolerance.

Professional Athletics

By 1957, the year in which *Fences* is set, black athletes had become an integrated part of professional and college sports, at least on the surface. The all-white teams of the World War II—and previous—years began to include blacks in 1947 when Jackie Robinson became the first black to play professional baseball since the color line was drawn in the 1890s. But the change still did not bring the same opportunity and equality as blacks might have hoped. Black leagues began to falter and disappear as more blacks began to support the now integrated ball teams. Troy Maxson, who had played in the Negro Leagues, found the change to integrated leagues had come too late; he was now too old to play professional ball.

The Negro Leagues had been financial disasters for players; salaries were inadequate to support a family. But, ten years after integration, the major leagues did not prove to be a financial bonanza for black players either. The huge salaries that were to become the hallmark of professional sports in the 1980s and 1990s simply did not exist in the late 1950s. The picture for college athletics was also different for blacks than for whites. Black players were not always permitted to live in campus housing, and when they traveled to games, black athletes were sometimes refused accommodations at hotels where the team was staying. Instead, black players were dropped off at the YMCA or lodged with black families. Given this knowledge, it is little wonder that Troy is suspicious of the recruiters who want to seduce his son with college scholarships and the possibility of a career in professional sports.

Employment

When the flood of immigrants poured into the United States at the beginning of the twentieth century, they found opportunity and employment in factories, offices, and small business. The white work force was plentiful and employers took advantage of the availability of the eager new citizens, who came expecting that hard work would make it possible to marry, raise a family, and live the American Dream. But for blacks, who were also moving into large northern cities in huge numbers, the American Dream remained an elusive possibility, just beyond their grasp.

Troy admits that had he not been able to use his brother's disability benefit, he would not have been able to purchase a home, even though he had been working hard for nearly twenty years. With the availability of a large white work force, blacks were too often the last hired and the first fired. In addition, many black workers lacked the training necessary to get ahead. The job of hauling garbage is available to blacks, but even within that job, there is a division of work by race. White employees drive trucks; black employees load the garbage. Troy cannot read and does not have a driver's license, but he breaks through the color barrier to win a driver's job because he complains that there are no black drivers. The union, which protects his job when he complains, is the one ally the black workers have.

Housing

Because of limited job opportunities, most blacks did not earn enough money to own their own homes. But in 1957 the American Dream became a reality for many white families. In the post-war economy, home ownership for whites was booming. The World War II G.I. bill had made it possible for returning servicemen to go to college. These better educated men found successful careers that brought a higher standard of living than the previous generation had known. This resulted in an explosion of new home building, the creation of suburbs, and ultimately, the exodus of whites from the inner city. Few blacks could afford the new homes that were going up on development sites all across the country. Instead, many urban blacks lived in the same kind of ghetto in which Wilson himself had been born. The front yard of the Maxson home is a rarity for most black families who often lived in huge inner-city apartment buildings.

Compare & Contrast

- **1957:** Ku Klux Klansmen accuse Alabama grocery-chain truck driver Willie Edwards, 25, of having made remarks to a white woman and force him at pistol point to jump to his death from the Tyler Goodwin Bridge into the Alabama River. It was Edwards's first day on the truck route.

  1985: Philadelphia police try to dislodge members of MOVE, an organization of armed blacks. They firebomb a house from the air on May 13 and the fire spreads to adjacent houses, killing 11 and leaving 200 homeless.

  Today: A black woman, previously on public assistance, organizes a million woman rally in Philadelphia. This variant on the 1996 million man march on Washington D.C. draws more than one million black women in a show of strength and solidarity.

- **1957:** The Motown Corporation is founded in Detroit, Michigan, by entrepreneur Barry Gordy Jr., 30, who invests $700 to start a recording company whose "Motown Sound" will figure large in popular music for more than two decades.

1985: *The Color Purple*, a film based on Alice Walker's novel, is a top grossing box office success for star Whoopi Goldberg and director Steven Spielberg.

Today: *Rosewood*, a film based on actual events that occurred in 1927, examines the massacre that destroyed a small Florida town after a white woman falsely accuses a black man of sexual assault.

- **1957:** Ghana becomes the first African state south of the Sahara to attain independence.

1985: South Africa declares a state of emergency July 20, giving police and the army almost absolute power in Black townships. The country's policy of apartheid has kept blacks as second-class citizens for decades.

Today: For the first time, South Africa is ruled by the racial majority (blacks) led by Nelson Mandela, who languished in white-run prisons during the last 27 years of apartheid rule.

- **1957:** The first U.S. civil rights bill since Civil War reconstruction days, passed by Congress September 9, establishes a Civil Rights Commission and provides federal safeguards for voting rights. Many Southerners oppose the bill.

1985: The Gramm-Rudman-Hollings Act signed by President Reagan mandates congressional spending limits in an effort to eliminate the federal deficit.

Today: Welfare reform results in a loss of services, including food stamps, public assistance, and medical care for many of the nation's poorest citizens. The reform is intended by politicians to be a mechanism that will force welfare recipients into the job force. But the change is seen by the many organizations that assist the poor as a misdirected effort that will punish the nation's already disadvantaged children.

Racism

The 1950s still revealed an America with two races, separated by color and economic barriers. Blacks and whites attended different schools, lived in different neighborhoods, and received different benefits from their citizenship. Before the advent of forced busing in the 1960s, most blacks attended schools in poorer neighborhoods. Because schools are funded by a complicated system of bonds supported by taxes, black schools (in neighborhoods that collected lower taxes) received less money and thus had smaller resources with which to pay salaries, maintain buildings, or buy new equipment. The result was that students at predominately black schools received a sub-standard level of education.

Other areas of inequality included suffrage and justice. Blacks were not encouraged to vote; in fact, many areas discouraged blacks from voting by instituting difficult competency exams as qualifiers. Whites were not required to pass these exams. Accordingly, blacks had little input into the political decisions that shaped their lives. Blacks also suffered unequal treatment under the law. Many could not read the contracts they signed or were too intimidated to protest. In addition, blacks often became the victims of discrimination under criminal statutes. Ignorance of their legal rights meant that blacks often languished in jail. In some cases, blacks were lynched by unruly mobs who were sometimes sanctioned by a law enforcement organization that looked the other way. The civil unrest of the 1960s was a direct result of these injustices.

Critical Overview

When *Fences* first opened on Broadway in March of 1987, Wilson had already spent four years in preproduction revisions to his play. James Earl Jones, who won a Tony Award for his performance in the Broadway production, had first played Troy Maxson in the Yale Repertory Theatre production two years earlier. His ease and interpretation of an already familiar character were evident to reviewers who hailed Jones's performance. Allan Wallach, in his *Newsday* review, said that Jones gave this role "its full measure of earthiness and complexity." Jones, said Wallach, was at his best when Troy is drinking and laughing with his friends; his "performance is at its heartiest in the bouts of drinking and bantering." Wallach also singled out Wilson's ability to capture the "rhythms of his characters" who gather in the yard of the Maxson home, a yard that "becomes a rich portrait of a man who scaled down his dreams to fit inside his run-down yard." Wallach's review is an acknowledgment of Wilson's strength in "depicting a black man forced to come to terms with an unfeeling white world." However, Wallach also found that the scenes where Troy interacts with his family sometimes fell to conventional family fare.

Reviewer Clive Barnes offered no such distinction in his review that appeared in the *New York Post*. Barnes called *Fences* a play that "seems to break away from the confines of art into a dense, complex realization of reality." *Fences* is a play that makes the audience forget it is in a theater, thinking instead that they are witnessing a real family drama. Barnes also singled out Jones for praise in a role that left the reviewer "transfixed." But Wilson was also praised for writing drama "so engrossing, so embracing, so simply powerful" that he transcended an effort to label him a black playwright. Instead, Wilson's ability to tell a story makes such labels, in Barnes's opinion, "irrelevant." Barnes also praised the play for its historic relevance and cited the lessons Troy learned while in prison and his experience playing baseball. Barnes declared that Wilson has created "the strongest, most passionate American dramatic writing since Tennessee Williams." Barnes's review contained no reservations. He praised the actors, noting that Jones's performance was not the only excellent one of the production and offered equal approval for the staging and setting. The sum total of these elements resulted in what Barnes described as "one of the richest experiences I have ever had in the theatre."

Edwin Wilson's praise of *Fences* was just as full of compliments as that of Barnes and Wallach. In his *Wall Street Journal* review, Wilson stated that with *Fences*, the author had demonstrated that he can "strike at the heart, not just of the black experience, but of the human condition." Troy is a character who is multi-dimensional; his complexity reveals a man "with the full measure of his shortcomings as well as his strengths." The audience witnesses the characters' depth of ambition, their frustration, and their pain, according to this reviewer. As did other reviewers, Wilson also noted the exceptional quality of the setting and the staging. *Fences*, said Wilson, is "an especially welcome and important addition to the season."

Sources

Barnes, Clive. "Fiery 'Fences'" in the *New York Post*, March 27, 1987.

Birdwell, Christine. "Death as a Fastball on the Outside Corner: *Fences*'s Troy Maxson and the American Dream" in *Aethlon: The Journal of Sport Literature*, Vol. 8, no. 1, Fall, 1990, pp. 87-96.

Ching, Mei-Ling. "Wrestling against History" in *Theater*, Vol. 19, no. 3, Summer-Fall, 1988, pp. 70-71.

DeVries, Hilary. "A Song in Search of Itself in *American Theatre*, Vol. 3, no. 10, January, 1987, pp. 22-25.

Elam, Harry J., Jr. "Of Angels and Transcendence: An Analysis of *Fences* by August Wilson and *Roosters* by Milcha Sanchez-Scott" in *Staging Difference: Cultural Pluralism in American Theatre and Drama*, edited by Marc Manfort, Peter Lang (New York), 1995, pp. 287-300.

Henderson, Heather. "Building *Fences:* An Interview with Mary Alice and James Earl Jones" in *Theater*, Vol. 16, no. 3, Summer-Fall, 1985, pp. 67-70.

Pereira, Kim. "August Wilson" in *Reference Guide to American Literature*, edited by Jim Kamp, third edition, St. James Press, 1994, pp. 919-21.

Shafer, Yvonne. "Breaking Barriers: August

Wilson" in *Staging Difference: Cultural Pluralism in American Theatre and Drama*, edited by Marc Manfort, Peter Lang, 1995. pp. 267-85.

Wallach, Allan. "Fenced in by a Lifetime of Resentments" in *Newsday*, March 27, 1987.

Wilson, Edwin. "Wilson's 'Fences' on Broadway" in the *Wall Street Journal*, March 31, 1987.

Further Reading

Chalk, Ocania. *Pioneers in Black Sport*, Dodd, Mead (New York), 1975.

> Chalk provides a detailed discussion of the complicated issue of integration in professional sports.

Elam, Harry J. "August Wilson's Women" in *May All Your Fences Have Gates*, University of Iowa Press, 1994.

> Elam is a Professor of Drama at Stanford University. This essay is an examination of the role of women in Wilson's dramas.

Elkins, Marilyn. *August Wilson: A Casebook*, Garland (New York), 1994.

> This narrow volume is a collection of essays that discuss Wilson's work within the context of historical and cultural influences.

Holway, John. *Voices from the Great Black Baseball Leagues*, Dodd, Mead, 1975.

> This is a scholarly investigation of the Negro Leagues based on player interviews and an examination of sports reportage.

In Their Own Words: Contemporary American Playwrights, Theatre Communications Group,

1988.

This essay is the transcript of a March 1987 interview with Wilson in which he discusses several of his plays.

Nadel, Alan. *Essays on the Drama of August Wilson*, University of Iowa Press (Iowa City), 1994

This is a collection of essays on Wilson's dramatic work. There is also a comprehensive bibliography included.

Paige, Leroy "Satchel." *Maybe I'll Pitch Forever*, Doubleday, 1962.

Perhaps the best-known player from the Negro baseball leagues, Satchel Paige is considered to be one of the finest players to engage the game of baseball. This book is an autobiographical look at his career in the Negro Leagues.

Rogosin, Donn. *Invisible Men: Life in Baseball's Negro Leagues*, Atheneum (New York), 1983.

This book offers an overview of the social issues that led to the end of the great Negro Leagues.

Ruck, Rob. *Sandlot Seasons: Sport in Black Pittsburgh*, University of Illinois Press (Urbana), 1987.

This nonfiction text probes the

history of sports in Pittsburgh, the
city of Wilson's youth and the model
for the urban setting of *Fences*.

Shannon, Sandra G. "The Ground on Which I
Stand" in *May All Your Fences Have Gates*,
University of Iowa Press, 1994.

Shannon is an Associate Professor of
English at Howard University. Her
essay examines the role of African
American women in Wilson's
dramas.